A New True Book

OCEANS

By Katharine Jones Carter

This "true book" was prepared
under the direction of
Illa Podendorf,
formerly with the Laboratory School,
University of Chicago

CHILDRENS PRESS, CHICAGO

California coast

PHOTO CREDITS
Tony Freeman—2, 4, 8, 10 (2 photos), 26 (right), 41 (right), 43, 44 (2 photos)
Shedd Aquarium, Patrice Ceisel, photographer—15 (3 photos), 22, 36 (left)
Lynn M. Stone—13, 16, 24, 26 (left), 28, 33, 37 (2 photos), 39, 40, 41 (left)
NOAA: National Oceanic and Atmospheric Administration—25 (Brian Chrisney photo), 34 (middle)
E. Webber-Cover
Ray Bruno—23
Len Meents—6, 20, 30
James P. Rowan—34 (top), 36 (right)
Marine Mammal Fund—34 (bottom)
Michael A. Rigsby—38
Alaska Division of Tourism—18
Cover—Atlantic Ocean

Library of Congress Cataloging in Publication Data

Carter, Katharine Jones, 1905-
    Oceans.

    (A New true book)
    Revised edition of: The true book of oceans. 1958.
    Summary: An introduction to the world's four largest bodies of salt water, the Atlantic, Pacific, Arctic, and Indian oceans.
    1. Ocean—Juvenile literature. [1. Ocean]
I. Title.
GC21.5.C37   1982   551.46   81-17093
ISBN 0-516-01639-3   AACR2

    12 13 14 15 16 17 18 19 20 R 99 98 97 96 95 94 93 92

TABLE OF CONTENTS

Oceans. . . 5

Floor. . . 21

Surface. . . 23

Shore. . . 26

Tides. . . 27

Currents. . . 29

Ocean Plants and Animals. . . 33

Ways the Ocean Helps Us. . . 39

Words You Should Know. . . 46

Index. . . 47

Oceans are the largest bodies of water.

OCEANS

There is more water than land in the world.

The largest bodies of water are called oceans.

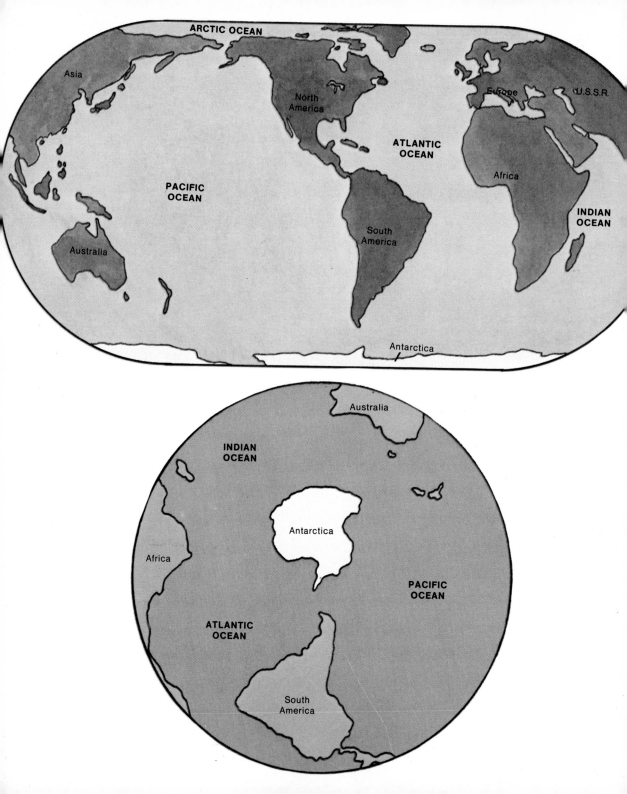

The names of the three biggest oceans are Pacific, Atlantic, and Indian. The waters of all three oceans meet around Antarctica. The waters of the Atlantic and Pacific oceans meet in the Arctic Ocean.

Ocean waters are salty.
Smaller bodies of salt
water are often called
seas.

Long ago people got salt for their food from the ocean.

Now we get it from salt mines. The mines are in places that were once covered by salt water. Now the water is gone. But it left tons of salt.

The oceans are different colors.

Usually they are shades of blue.

In very cold parts of the world, the ocean is green.

The green color comes, in part, from tiny creatures that find it easy to live in cold waters.

In one place, tiny living things make the water so red that it is called the Red Sea.

The Indian Ocean is such a dark blue that it is sometimes called black.

Storm over the Gulf of Mexico

Storm clouds give the ocean a gray-green color. Muddy rivers make an ocean yellow-brown where they flow into it.

Most parts of the oceans are deep. In some places, the oceans are deeper than a mountain is high.

In some places, the oceans are warm. A tropical sun beats down on the water, day after day.

Above left: Striped
           puffer

Above: Clown anenome fish

Left: Longnosed
      hawkfish

Fish with beautiful colors
live in the warm ocean
waters.

Icebergs in Hudson Bay, Canada

In some places, the oceans are cold. Mountain-like pieces of ice float in the water.

These are called icebergs.

Glacier Bay, Alaska

Icebergs are made by glaciers. Glaciers are streams of ice hundreds of feet thick. They do not seem to move. But this ice flows slowly from the tops of the mountains to the oceans. Waves and tides break off great chunks of ice that float away as icebergs.

Islands often are the tops of undersea mountains.

FLOOR

The bottom of the ocean
is called the floor.
There are hills,
mountains, and valleys on
the floor of the oceans.
There are rocks, shells,
and fish, too.

Sunlight does not reach the floor where the ocean is very deep. It is so dark that no plants can grow there.

Some of the fish can make their own light. Parts of their bodies glow in the dark.

Flashlight fish

SURFACE

The top of the ocean is called the surface.

Many fish live near the surface of the oceans.

Some of the smallest plants and animals in the world live near the surface waters, too.

All sea animals find their food in the water around them.

Wind blowing against the surface of the ocean makes waves.

In a strong wind, the waves rise and push forward. The white bubbling foam on top of a wave is called a whitecap.

When a wave rolls over on itself, it is a breaker.

Giant waves are sometimes taller than a ship. They have great power. They can pound a ship to pieces against the rocks in a storm.

SHORE

Where the surface of the ocean touches the land, there is a shore or coast.

There are rocky shores.

There are flat shores covered with sand.

These are beaches.

TIDES

The oceans are always moving toward the land, or away from it. This "coming in" and "going out" is called tides.

Tides are different from waves.

Tides are the whole body of water moving slowly toward the land, or slowly away from it.

Tides are caused by the moon and sun pulling water toward them.

When the water moves toward the shore, it is a flood tide.

When the water moves away from the shore, it is an ebb tide.

There are two flood tides and two ebb tides in a day and a night.

Kelp bed at low tide or ebb tide

CURRENTS

There are two kinds of river-like streams in the ocean.

These streams are called currents. They are caused by the wind and turning of the earth.

Some currents flow through surface waters of the oceans.

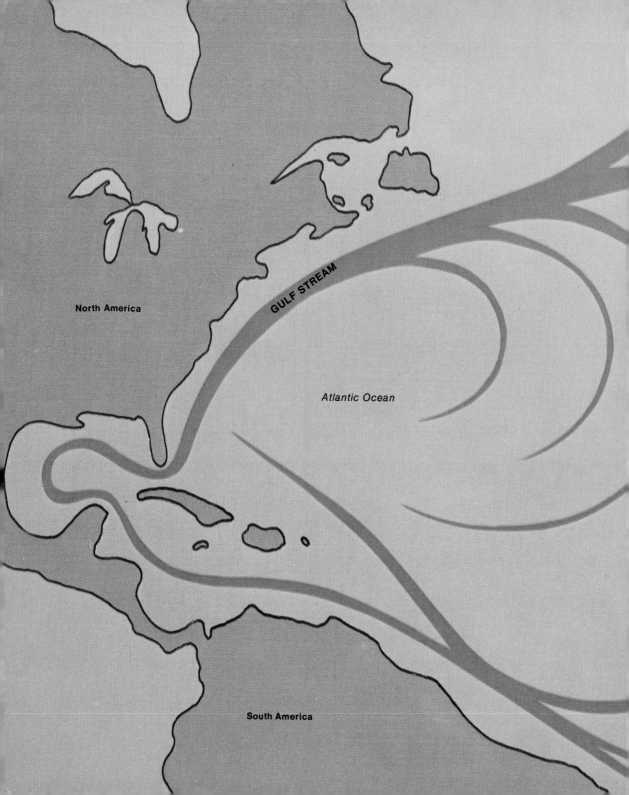

North America

GULF STREAM

Atlantic Ocean

South America

Some currents move toward the surface or away from it.

Most currents are hard to see. But one has a color of its own. This is the Gulf Stream in the Atlantic Ocean.

From an airplane, the Gulf Stream looks like a blue river moving through a green ocean.

The Gulf Stream is warm water.

As it passes close to some land, it brings warm weather.

Other currents bring cool weather to the land they flow near.

Atlantic blue crab

OCEAN PLANTS AND ANIMALS

The oceans are full of life.

Some of the biggest living things and some of the smallest live in the oceans.

Harbor seal

Lobster

Blue whale
blowing

Whales and fur seals like the cold ocean water.

Fishermen get cod and sardines from cold water.

Fishermen go to warmer water for tuna. There are thousands of kinds of fish in the oceans.

Sponges are found in almost every ocean. They are animals that fasten themselves to rocks or shells on the ocean floor.

Above: Brown pelican
Left: Humboldt's penguin

They take their food from the water that flows through them.

Penguins swim in the cold ocean water to look for their food. Most penguins live in Antarctica.

Pelicans dive for food in warmer ocean waters.

Above: Steamer clams
Right: Great black-backed gull

Sea gulls live along the ocean shores.

Many kinds of shellfish live near the shore.

Seaweeds are plants that grow in ocean waters. Some are almost too small to be seen. Some grow hundreds of feet long.

Seaweeds have no roots,
stems, or leaves. Some
kinds of seaweed look like
long strings of brown
grass. Blue, green, or red
seaweeds grow in some
ocean waters.

Many animals eat
seaweeds.

WAYS THE OCEAN HELPS US

The ocean gives us food.
We get about two
hundred different kinds of
fish for food from the
ocean.

Salmon fleet, Alaska

Clam diggers in Cape Cod Bay

We dig clams from the mud at ebb tide.

We rake up oysters from shallow waters.

We get cod-liver oil from the cod, and whale oil from the whale.

An ocean is beautiful. It gives us pleasure in many ways.

We can swim in it, and boat on it, and watch it come and go.

We get a medicine, iodine, from kelp, a seaweed.

Fertilizer is made from certain kinds of seaweeds. Fertilizer is a food for the farmers' land.

It helps plants to grow.

The oceans are like
broad highways. Little
boats, big boats, working
boats, and pleasure boats
sail the ocean.

Many of them go across the ocean from one country to another.

Oceans are beautiful to see. They give many creatures a place to live. They give us food. They help us in many ways.

Oceans are an important part of our world.

WORDS YOU SHOULD KNOW

breaker(BRAIK • er) — a wave that breaks into foam when it reaches the shore.

broad(BRAWD) — wide; large from side to side

chunk — a thick piece

clam — a water animal that has a soft body and a shell with two parts

coast — the edge of the land touching the sea

cod — a kind of fish

creature(KREE • cher) — a living being

current(KER • ent) — the movement of water

ebb tide — when the water moves out from the shore

Emperor penguin(EM • per • rer PEN • gwin) — one of the largest of the penguins

fasten(FASS • en) — to attach

fertilizer(FER • tih • lye • zer) — something added to soil to make it better for growing plants

foam(FOME) — a mass of tiny bubbles

flood tide(FLUD TYDE) — when the water moves into the shore

glacier(GLAY • sher) — a large mass of ice that moves slowly down a valley or mountain

iceberg(ICE • berg) — a large mass of floating ice in the ocean

iodine(EYE • oh • dine) — one of the chemical elements

kelp — a brown seaweed

oyster(OIE • ster) — a sea animal that has a soft body and a shell with two parts

pelican(PEL • ih • kin) — a large bird with a long bill and webbed feet

power — force; able to do work

sardine — a small fish

sea — a body of salt water; ocean

seaweed — plants that live in the ocean

shallow(SHAL • oh) — not deep

shellfish (SHELL • fish) — a water animal that has a shell as an
outer covering

shore — land that touches the water

sponge (SPUNJ) — a water animal that grows and lives under water

surface (SIR • fiss) — the top

tide — change in the level of oceans and other large bodies of water
caused by the pull of the moon and sun on the earth

tropical (TROP • ih • kil) — hot and damp

tuna — a large ocean fish that is used for food

valley — land between hills or mountains

white-cap — the foam on top of a wave

animals of the ocean, 23, 24, 35-38

Antarctica, 7, 36

Arctic Ocean, 7

Atlantic Ocean, 7, 31

beaches, 26

biggest oceans, 7

black colored ocean, 12

blue colored oceans, 11

boats, 43

breaker waves, 25

clams, 40

coasts, 26

cod, 35, 40

cod-liver oil, 40

cold oceans, 17, 35, 36

colors of currents, 31

colors of oceans, 11-13

currents, 29-32

darkness, at ocean's floor, 22

depth of oceans, 14, 22

ebb tides, 28, 40

fertilizer, 42

fish, 15, 21, 22, 23, 35, 39

flood tides, 28

floor of the ocean, 21, 22, 35

food, 39

fur seals, 35

glaciers, 19

gray-green oceans, 13

green colored oceans, 11, 31

Gulf Stream, 31, 32

icebergs, 17, 19

Indian Ocean, 7, 12

iodine, 42

kelp, 42

medicine, 42

moon, 27

mountains on ocean floor, 21
oysters, 40
Pacific Ocean, 7
pelicans, 36
penguins, 36
plants, 22, 23, 37, 42
pleasure, from oceans, 41
Red Sea, 12
rivers, 13
rocks, 21, 35
salt, 8, 9
salt mines, 9
salt water, 9
sardines, 35
sea animals, 23, 24, 35-38
sea gulls, 37
seals, 35
seas, 8
seaweeds, 37, 38, 42
shellfish, 37
shells, 21, 35
shores, 26, 37
sponges, 35
storms, 13, 25
streams in oceans, 29-32
sun, 14, 22, 27
surface of the ocean, 23-25, 26, 29, 31
tides, 27, 28, 40
tuna, 35
valleys on ocean floor, 21
warm currents, 32
warm oceans, 14, 15, 35, 36
waves, 24, 25
whale oil, 40
whales, 35, 40
whitecaps, 24
wind, 24, 29
yellow-brown oceans, 13

About the Author

Katherine Carter's long association with elementary students ended with her retirement from the Baltimore school system. Her move to a home on the shore of the Piankatank River fulfilled a lifetime dream. Mrs. Carter and her husband enjoy fishing, crabbing, gardening and reading.